UGLY ANIMALS

D1488948

Komodo Dragons

Kerri O'Donnell

PowerKiDS press.

New York

Published in 2007 by The Rosen Publishing Group, Inc.
29 East 21st Street, New York, NY 10010

Book Design: Michael Ruberto

Library of Congress Cataloging-in-Publication Data

O'Donnell, Kerri, 1972-
  Komodo dragons / Kerri O'Donnell.
     p. cm. - (Ugly animals)
  Includes index.
  ISBN 13: 978-1-4358-3832-1

  1. Komodo dragon-Juvenile literature. I. Title.
  QL666.L29O36 2007
  597.95'968-dc22

                          2006015704

Manufactured in the United States of America

Contents

That's a Big, Ugly Lizard!

Komodo dragons are the biggest lizards in the world. The biggest male Komodos can grow to be over 10 feet (3 m) long and weigh 365 pounds (166 kg)!

It is easy to see why Komodos are called dragons. They have big bodies, lots of sharp teeth, and forked tongues. Just like dragons in fairy tales, Komodos can seem very scary. They will eat any animal they can sink their teeth into—even other Komodos!

When a Komodo dragon sticks out its long tongue, it almost looks like it is breathing fire.

Dragon Legends

Komodo dragons live on a few small islands in the Flores Sea. These islands are part of Indonesia, a country in the Indian Ocean. Scientists around the world only found out about Komodo dragons in 1912. The people who lived on the islands knew about the giant lizards for hundreds of years. They told travelers about them, but no one believed them! When scientists began traveling to the small islands, they learned that Komodos were real and not just **legends**.

A Komodo's tongue helps it "smell" dead animals from several miles (km) away.

Once upon a Time . . .

The **ancestors** of Komodo dragons were probably smaller lizards that came to the islands from Australia more than a million years ago. They swam from island to island when ocean levels were low during an **ice age**. The islands were also connected at certain times long ago.

When the ice age ended, water levels rose again. The lizards were left on the islands. There were few animals to hunt them there. Over time, the lizards grew bigger and stronger eating the other island animals.

Komodo dragons are ver
strong swimmers, eve
though they spend mos
of their time on land

Living with the Heat

The islands where the Komodos live are very hot and dry. Like all **reptiles**, Komodo dragons are **cold-blooded**. In the morning, they sit in the sun to warm up. When they get too hot, Komodos rest in **burrows** or in the shade. At night, they often sleep in burrows.

Komodos can go without water for days. If they are thirsty, they will gulp down large amounts of water at a time.

Komodos usually dig their own burrows, but they also take over burrows from other animals, such as porcupines.

Fighters and Hunters

Komodo dragons are a kind of lizard called a monitor. All monitors are meat-eaters and excellent hunters. Komodos are very strong and often fight with each other. They don't like to share food. Komodos use their strength, speed, and size to catch **prey**. They have strong jaws and sharp teeth. Komodos sometimes bite the legs of their prey to bring them down. They might also use their claws to bring prey down. Then they use their teeth to tear the prey apart.

Komodos can run 12 miles (19 km) per hour for short periods of time

Come and Get It!

Komodos spend much of their time hunting for food. They eat any animal they can catch. Komodos hide near paths that animals use. They wait for an animal to pass by, then jump out and bite it. The Komodo has **venom** that can make other animals very sick. If the animal gets away, the Komodo often catches up to the sick animal. It will then kill the animal and eat it.

This Komodo dragon will use its teeth to tear off chunks of the deer's flesh and bones. Komodos swallow without chewing

Komodo Eggs

Female Komodos lay fifteen to thirty eggs once a year, usually in September. They lay their eggs in U-shaped burrows that they dig in sandy soil. Komodo parents don't take care of the eggs, and they don't take care of their young once the eggs **hatch**.

Komodo dragons hatch after 8 or 9 months, at the end of the islands' rainy season. This way there is plenty of water for the young Komodos to drink after they are born.

Komodo dragons have to be careful when they choose a place to lay their eggs. Other Komodo dragons will eat the eggs if they find them.

Life in the Trees

Baby Komodos are between 10 and 22 inches (25 and 56 cm) long. Adult Komodos are dull gray in color. Young Komodos can be a mix of brown, yellow, orange, red, and green with black and white marks.

Young Komodos live in trees to stay safe from enemies, including adult Komodos. They eat bugs, birds, snakes, and other animals they hunt in the trees. They live in trees until they are big enough to protect themselves from adult Komodos.

By the time they are a year and a half old Komodos have nearly doubled in size

Living with Dragons

Komodos spend most of their time alone. However, if a Komodo kills an animal or finds a dead one, many other Komodos may come to join the feast. If the animal isn't big enough to feed all of the Komodos, the dragons may fight over it.

Komodos must keep themselves safe from other animals, too. Dogs, birds, snakes, and wild cats will attack and eat young Komodos if they have the chance.

Komodos have been known to attack a person who is not paying attention or is weak or sick. It is best to stay away from Komodo dragons.

Saving the Dragons

Today, there are only about 5,000 Komodo dragons left in the wild. They are in danger of becoming **extinct**.

The government of Indonesia has set up a safe place for Komodos to live called Komodo National Park. This park includes several islands. The largest is called Komodo Island. Zoos around the world are also learning how to care for Komodos so they don't disappear forever.

Glossary

ancestor (AN-sehs-tuhr) A relative from long ago.

burrow (BUHR-oh) A small, tight space in the ground made
   by digging.

cold-blooded (KOHLD–BLUH-duhd) Describing an animal
   that is as cold or as warm as its surroundings.

extinct (ihk-STINKT) No longer existing.

hatch (HACH) To come out of an egg.

ice age (EYS AYJ) A long period of time when ice covered
   much of Earth's surface.

legend (LEH-juhnd) A story that hasn't been proven and
   seems impossible.

prey (PRAY) An animal that is hunted by other animals as food.

reptile (REHP-tyl) An animal that is usually covered with
   scales, such as an alligator or a lizard. A reptile is as warm
   or as cold as the air around it.

venom (VEH-nuhm) A poison that some animals make in their
   bodies that is harmful to other animals.

Index

Web Sites

Due to the changing nature of Internet links, PowerKids Press has developed an online list of Web sites related to the subject of this book. This site is updated regularly. Please use this link to access the list:
http://www.powerkidslinks.com/uglyani/komodo/